TITS & ASS

TITS

A GUIDE TO THE ANIMAL KINGDOM'S RUDEST RESIDENTS

& ASS

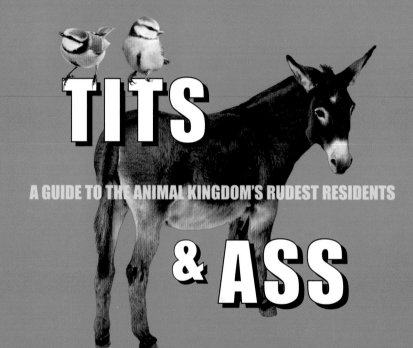

DOG 'N' BONE

Published in 2012 by Dog 'n' Bone Books

An imprint of Ryland Peters & Small Ltd

20–21 Jockey's Fields   519 Broadway, 5th Floor
London WC1R 4BW   New York, NY 10012

www.dogandbonebooks.com

10 9 8 7 6 5 4 3 2 1

A CIP catalog record for this book is
available from the Library of Congress
and the British Library.

ISBN: 978 0 957140 90 5

Printed in China

Editor: Franklin J. Barker
Designer: Dawn Keebles
Photography credits: see page 64

For digital editions, visit
www.cicobooks.com/apps.php

CONTENTS

Introduction

Animals, they are my life. They are my inspirations, they are my *raison d'etre*, they are my passion—I love them all. It may sound silly to some, but I wake up every morning thinking about cocks and go to bed at night to dream about ass. I just can't get enough!

I'm lucky enough to have a job that allows me to get up close and personal with tits, get my hands on aholes, and indulge my love for shags on an almost daily basis. In fact, I adore shags so much some might even consider me an addict... and I'll hold my hands up to say, "Guilty as charged!" I've stroked every rat, beaver, camel toe, and pecker that I've ever come across and I still want more. In my personal life I own a whole menagerie of furry and feathered friends. If I had to pick a favorite from my collection I'd struggle, but maybe would go for cats. I've lost count of the amount of pussy I've had over the years, but believe me it's a lot! Black, white, ginger... they've all come back to my place at one time or another.

It was my deep bond with the animal kingdom that led me to put together this book, which aims to outline the prejudices, challenges, and misrepresentations that face the natural world every day. If you thought it was just environmental threats that animals are subject to, you'd be wrong. They also face vicious verbal attacks. Day by day, innocent animals' names are being misused in lewd, objectionable, and obscene ways. Years ago a bear was a bear, now it has all sorts of connotations that the *Ursus actos* could never have imagined whilst minding its own business in the great outdoors. A beautiful cougar never wanted to associated with predatory females, at least not of the human kind, but that is what has happened. So I've decided to take affirmative action and reiterate that while some words have evolved way beyond their original meanings, the original animals are still here and demand respect.

I'd like to thank you for taking the time to read my work and would like to leave you with one final statement, which I hope reflects what I aim to get across by writing this book: hooray for boobies!

Dr Robert Tiergarten

cock [kok]

n.
1. male chicken: *The farmer's wife had seen many cocks in her time*
2. male bird in general
3. slang: vulgar. penis
4. slang: offensive. blockhead or idiot

pussy [poos-ee]

n. (pl) *pussies*
1. affectionate term for a cat or kitten
2. slang. a person lacking courage
3. slang: vulgar. the vulva

see also
pussy willow
n.
1. American tree with furry flowers

shag [shag]

n.
1. New Zealand sea bird
2. matted, coarse hair
3. slang: vulgar. vagina

v. (used without object)
1. British slang. to have sexual intercourse

booby [boo-bee]

n. (pl) *boobies*

1. seabird closely related to the gannet, often with colored feet or bill: *There are some fine-looking boobies on the beach today*
2. a person lacking in intelligence
3. slang: often vulgar. breasts

see also

tits (page 32)

BOOBY

beaver [bee-ver]

n.
1. a water-dwelling rodent: *That beaver is sopping wet*
2. slang: vulgar. vagina

v. (used without object)
1. British. to work hard

BEAVER

RAT

rat [rat]

n.

1. rodent animal from the family Muroidea
2. slang. rogue, rapscallion, scallywag
3. slang. someone who breaks trust or informs against an associate
4. slang: vulgar. vagina: *Get your rat out*

v. (used without object)

1. slang. to inform against someone or betray them: *The factory worker decided to rat on his manager for eating the cheese*

GOATSUCKER

goatsucker [goht-suhk-er]

n.

1. nightjar, a medium-sized nocturnal bird
2. slang. a thoroughly unpleasant person of little to no morals: *That goatsucker is so filthy he could take a bath for a week and still come out dirty*

see also

hogsucker (page 46)

horny toad [haw-nee tohd]

n.

1. desert horned lizard found in North America, actually a lizard rather than a toad

2. slang: offensive. low-life individual cursed with an higher than average libido or person who repulses: *On my way home I had the misfortune of meeting a horny toad looking to make my acquaintance*

HORNY TOAD

dik-dik [dik-dik]

n.

1. small antelope approx. 20–28 inches in height

2. slang: vulgar. penis (as said by a person with a stutter)

note

Female dik-diks are usually larger than males, but the males have horns. The dik-dik has a gland that secretes a sticky fluid used for scent marking purposes.

DIK-DIK

bitch [bich]

n. (pl) *bitches*

1. female dog, wolf, or fox

2. slang: offensive. derogatory term used to
   describe someone, esp. a woman

3. slang: offensive. person who is involved in
   a subservient relationship with another
   person or group: *Following her demand,
   John baked another cupcake with sprinkles for
   Sandra as he was her bitch*

v. (used without object)

1. slang: to register dissatisfaction about
   something or someone: *John bitched to his
   colleague about Sandra. He considered her to be
   a total bitch*

27

ass [as]

n. (pl) *asses*

1. donkey closely related to the horse family:
   Have you seen that ass over there? It is huge

2. person suffering from a deficiency of
   brain cells

3. slang: vulgar. posterior or backside
   of a human or animal

see also

esp. British. arse [ahs]

clam [klam]

n.

1. bivalve mollusc
2. slang: vulgar. vagina

v. (used without object)
to clam up

1. slang. to go quiet or be unwilling to discuss something

see also
clam snacker [klam snak-er]
n.

1. person who eats clams
2. someone who performs the act of cunnilingus

CLAM

tits [tits]

n.

1. shortened form of titmice, North American birds

2. British. name for small birds from the family Paridae

3. slang: vulgar. mammary glands: *When Carl the hungry baby was presented with his mother's tits, he replied, "Thanks for the mammories"*

4. slang (sing): chiefly British. a simpleton

TITS

HONKERS

honkers [hong-khers]

n.

1. informal. a flock of geese
2. someone or something who makes a honking sound
3. slang: vulgar. breasts

see also

honk [hongk]

v. (used without object)

1. slang: chiefly British. to smell of something: *Those bitches honk of fish, I wonder where they have been?*
2. to make a honking sound
3. slang. to vomit

bangus [bang-uhs]

n. (pl) *banguses*

1. colloquial term in Southeast Asia esp. the Philippines for a boneless milkfish: *I went to Manila and there were lots of people in the streets yelling "Bangus, please"*

2. request, usually from excited females at a Justin Bieber concert

BANGUS

crappie [krap-ee]

n.

1. freshwater fish found in North American rivers, comes in black or white varieties, depending on what they have eaten: *Would you look at that black crappie, what strange coloring; they must have eaten something unusual*

adj., *-pier*, *-piest*

1. slang. poorly made
2. slang. terrible, awful, unenjoyable

CRAPPIE

bear [bare]

n.

1. animal from the family Ursidae
2. slang. used by the LGBT community to describe a large, hirsute male who is rugged in appearance and often portrays a highly masculine persona: *Upon entering the club John realised he was in bear country*

v. (used with object)

1. to support
2. to carry
3. to possess
4. to give birth to or produce

camel toe [kam-ul toh]

n.

1. forefoot of a camel: *The tourists were shocked by the size of the camel toe on display; none had seen one so pronounced before*

2. slang: vulgar. impression of the *mons pubis* or labia made on a particularly tight item of clothing

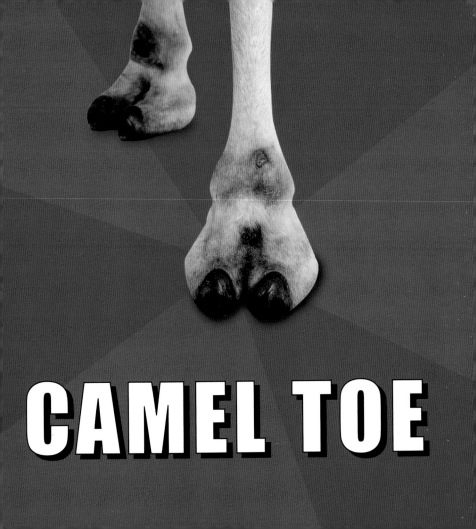

CAMEL TOE

ram [ram]

n.

1. uncastrated male sheep or goat
2. object used to force something open or break something down

v. (used with object)

1. to force something open or break something down
2. to force something into a confined space: *On rainy days the farmer liked to ram his sheep in the barn*
3. slang: vulgar. to engage in intercourse

RAM

HOGSUCKER

hogsucker [hawg-suk-er]

n.

1. type of fish from the sucker fish family
   that feeds on bottom dwelling organisms.
   Usually found in North American rivers

2. slang: offensive. insult accusing the
   recipient of having loose-enough
   morals to consider performing fellatio
   on a member of the genus Sus, or pig

cougar [coo-ger]

n.

1. member of the cat family found across North, Central, and South America

see also

mountain lion

puma

panther

2. slang. predatory older female who actively targets younger men or women for relations of a sexual nature: *That cougar is going to hunt that boy down and teach him a lesson*

COUGAR

ahole [a-hohl]

n.

1. alternative name for the adult Hawaiian flagtail fish found in the Pacific Ocean around the islands of Hawaii

2. slang. shortened and less offensive version of the word asshole, meaning an ignoble or despicable member of society

see also

ass (page 28)

asshole

AHOLE

PECKER

pecker [pek-er]

n.

1. woodpecker: *John's pecker had the most extraordinary coloring*
2. something or someone who pecks
3. slang: vulgar. appendage of a male

GRUNTER

grunter [gruhn-ter]

n.

1. fish that are members of the family Terapontidae found in the Pacific and Indian Oceans

2. someone or something that emits a grunting noise esp. pigs

3. slang. a person who is excessively flatulent: *One of life's least pleasurable experiences is being stuck in a confined space with a grunter*

worm [wuhm]

n.

1. long-bodied invertebrate without an exoskeleton
2. sly, underhanded, duplicitous person
3. slang. penis, usually of the tiny variety

v. (used without object)

1. to use questionable or disingenuous methods to accomplish a goal

WORM

chub [chub]

n.

1. freshwater fish found in Europe and North American lakes and rivers. Species include the fat chub, bigeye chub, and hornyhead chub: *Did you see that bear put that chub in its mouth*

2. slang: vulgar. erect penis

see also

chubby (pl) *chubbies*

1. overweight man who is part of a subculture of the gay community

CHUB

bone [bohn]

n.

1. part of an animal or human skeleton

v. (used with object)

1. slang: vulgar. to engage in intercourse with another: *Cedric like to bone his friend on Tuesdays after football practice*

2. to take bones out of a piece of meat or fish

see also

boner

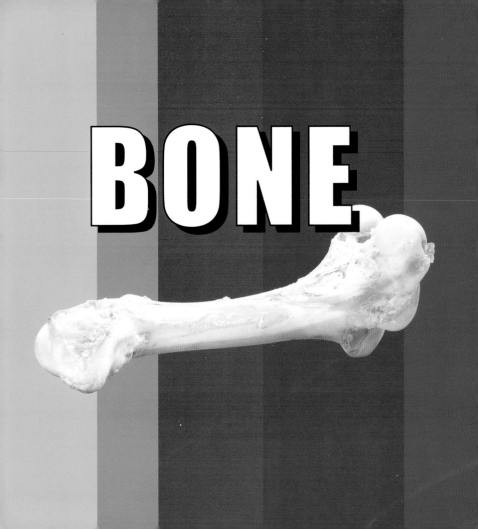

udders [uhd-ers]

n.

1. mammary gland of an animal, particularly ruminants including goats and cows

2. slang: vulgar. breasts: *Her malfunctioning bra led to scenes of udder chaos*

picture credits
[pik-cher kred-its]

All images © Getty Images except:

1. Alamy © pages 23, 39
2. iStock Photo © pages 37, 54
3. Corbis © page 46